This Sweet Haphazard

This Sweet Haphazard

gillian wegener

poems

Sixteen Rivers Press

Copyright © 2017 by Gillian Wegener
All rights reserved
Printed in the United States of America

Published by Sixteen Rivers Press
P.O. Box 640663
San Francisco, CA 94164-0663
www.sixteenrivers.org

Library of Congress Control Number: 2016950519
ISBN: 978-1-939639-13-4

Design: Marian Martino

Cover art: Night and Day Door, *Gillian Wegener, photograph*

For Sophia,

my hometown girl,

and

Ken Wegener,

my father

(1937–2016)

Contents

We Live Here

- Red Velvet Mite 3
- Chorus 4
- Old Mill Cafe 5
- Scene with Lake and Bees 7
- The Sign Said Nirvana 8
- America by Train 10
- And so, in spring 11
- After Dry Lightning 13
- Myriad Trees on Strange Mountains 14
- Solitary 15
- July Fourth 17
- Distraction, Furious and Brief 18
- Neville Bros. Service 19
- House for Sale 20
- 16 Reasons You Shouldn't Like Me 22
- The Streets Are Quiet Here Early Mornings 25
- A Boy Comes Toward You 26
- Alphabet for a Mid-Sized City 27

Avenue of the Giants, Auto Tour

- Stop No. 8: The Drury-Chaney Loop 33
- Stop No. 7: Chandler Grove 34
- Stop No. 6: Dyerville Overlook 35
- The Dyerville Giant 36
- Stop No. 5: Mahan Plaque 37
- Nature Walk 38
- Stop No. 4: Weott 39
- Drive-Thru Tree, Myersville 40
- Stop No. 3: Visitors' Center/Burlington Campground 41
- Between Stops 42
- Stop No. 2: Bolling Grove 43
- Stop No. 1: Franklin K. Lane Grove 44

Neighborhood

Neighborhood 47

The Moon Rises, Almost Full

New Life with Bees and Fire 59
7 Fieldstone Drive 60
My Father Begins to Disappear 61
Photo of Two Sisters, 1975 62
Owl Sighting 63
Later Stages 65
Empty Garden 66
Miró's *Women and Bird in the Moonlight* 67
Flood 68
The Big One 69
Birdsong 71
Father-Daughter Dance: A Ghazal 72
Astronomy for Mother and Daughter 73
Letter to My Husband Far Away 74
Road Song, North on 99 75
My Autopsy 77
This Sweet Haphazard 80

Notes 83
Acknowledgments 85

We Live Here

Red Velvet Mite

Smaller than a period on the page,
you moved up the poem, orange-red,
legs so small I couldn't make them out.
You would not cross a letter, but
sought the empty spaces, skirting
the low loop of a *g* and gliding
between the word *folding* and the word
hills, crevasses to the minute you.
You, spidery, skittered up to the next line
and passed between the *a* and the *s* in *grass*,
your hike slowing only when you changed
direction to avoid the black curves that must
have seemed . . . mysterious? dangerous?
You tested a comma, then backed away,
kept going, up to the top stanza, the first line,
into the wide white safety between poem
and title, and then I looked away—
the light was golden and green,
caught high in the trees—looked back,
and you were gone, the page just a poem,
the poem made up of words, the words
made up of letters that were to you
the deepest of deep unknowns.

Chorus

Listen: there are those of us from somewhere else,
the names of birthplaces, of hometowns,
under our skin, tattoos always felt, never seen.
We live here now, though we always meant to leave.

And there are those of us who were born here,
passing the landmarks of our lives so often
we don't think about them. We never meant to stay.
This place was marked as *just for now*, as *stepping stone*,
as *temporary* on our well-drawn maps.
But for one reason or another, years pass
and we find ourselves hot-stepping with jobs and kids
and this and that and a million little possessions.

Now, the kids say they want to move away. They point
their faces the same directions our faces used to point.
We'll let them go, of course, knowing more of them
than they think will come back, and that various wayfarers
too will stop for lunch and find themselves
staying for years' worth of dinners. They will all
find themselves here with the earth spreading
out around them, whispering a welcome
they will be more than a little surprised to hear.

The Old Mill Cafe

Everyone knew where to sit.
Everyone knew what time the men from the dairy plant came in after the
    night shift.
Everyone knew when the all-night drunks would come looking for breakfast.
Everyone knew when Sandy's girl ran away and why.
Everyone knew the size of the pancakes.
Everyone knew the windmill might really work, but then again, who could
    be sure.
Everyone knew when the junior college let out for summer.
Everyone knew when the talk was that the highway would be decommissioned.
Everyone knew when the hometown boy made good.
Everyone knew when the waitress was home sick and that she wasn't sick at all.
Everyone knew and everyone commented when something wasn't right.
Some folks commented with words and more words, and some just nodded,
    and some didn't nod.
Everyone knew that team didn't deserve to win that championship game.
Everyone knew the goddamned hippies weren't welcome.
Everyone knew the smell of fresh coffee and the little clanks of the
    creamer lids.
Everyone left that stool empty for a long time after Charlie passed.
Everyone clutched their coffee cups when the train passed through—
    could have touched the train as it squeezed by—the truth then, but
        not now.
Everyone heard about the accident, and then everyone knew or thought
    they knew.
Everyone knew wind from the west meant a little rain.
No one knew what happened to that kid who used to bus tables.
Everyone knew when the price of almonds just about dropped through
    the floor.
Everyone knew the overpass was coming and that the Old Mill would be razed.
Everyone knew the café would reopen way down the street, and no one was

happy about it.
Everyone knew they would keep going to the new place, which they did even though it wasn't the same—eggs tasted different, couldn't put a finger on it.
Everyone knew that things don't stay the same, and there's no use in whining about any of it.

Scene with Lake and Bees

Two men stand knee-deep in lake water,
lake at their backs, in front of them
lakeshore, feeble beach made of rock and dust,
some mud between the *lap-lap* of the water
and the *hush-hush* of mothers with toddlers—
tired, the mothers and the toddlers, from the day
that has spun itself around them and wrapped
them up in a gold-dust cocoon and dropped
them here, chrysalised, in late afternoon.
The men stand knee-deep in lake water
and survey the scene—Act IV, Scene 3:
a string of bees, stage right, hovering over sand
in one of the mucky spots between rocks.
The bees hang there as if dangled, bob up
and down, don't really move much,
land on the sand, then alight. *Honeybees*,
one of the men says. An inch here, an inch there.
Any movement almost mechanical.
No, meat bees, says the other.
The water laps at their knees
with little *kiss-kiss* sounds. The water
treats the rocks the same way. The sun
touches the tops of trees, and the mothers
begin shaking out their blankets as if they
were new, damp wings. The bees,
wearing their tiny black and yellow costumes,
get what they can from the sand. The men wade
out of the water and into the dust. The lake
is not sorry to see them go. She'll take her
curtain call for tonight in an hour or two,
then let the moonlight have its way.

The Sign Said Nirvana

The Buick belonged to the palm reader
and her erstwhile husband, the essayist.
That's their imprints on the seats.
That's their coffee stain.
Now, the tires fail slowly.
Rats take cover under the hood,
rats with those naked, scaly tails.
But take note, friend. Take heart.
All ghosts and rats were chased out last week
with a super-vac and some Rat-B-Gone.
1968 was a good year for some, but
only some. Everyone else placed their bets
and put up buildings made of corrugated metal.
Everyone else tried to make a decent living.
At noon now, the mechanic hides out
in the Buick's backseat.
He's drinking a Coke.
He's reading Travis McGee.
He's thinking of heading to Florida.
The light backhanding off the building
makes a good light for reading, but
is nothing like the sexy light of Florida.
Can you make a decent living there?
What's the ratio of metal buildings to mechanics?
Damn 1968 with its flowers and its astronauts.
The sideview mirror's broken out, the rearview's missing,
so there's no telling what's coming:
ghosts trying to wheedle their way back in,
rats figuring, what the hell, just go.
Just go, mutters the mechanic, *to Florida,*
to Galveston, to anywhere but here,

while the tires on the getaway car slowly deflate
and the palm reader's erstwhile essayist
drifts by on foot, ever regretful, thinking,
She should've seen this coming, she should've known,
she should've spoken up and said,
Honey, let's hit the wide-open road.

America by Train

America passes by the window like a set of slides being shown too fast. Here are the desert scenes with long stretches of blank landscape, but you know that it's all in the details. How the gray-green cactus will open up the most beautiful pink flower for just one day, but you'll never see that flower from this train window. How the lizard will wait on its rock for the unfortunate cricket to land and become a tiny meal. You won't hear the screech of the hawk welcoming sunset or see the startle of the mouse in hearing that cry. What you can see is brown and gray and vaguely green, with the wide, darkening sky overhead, and it's like holding a book you know will be a good read but that you aren't allowed to open.

But here are the passengers, their unchosen details out for display. The man and wife who argue about every little thing in hard whispers and then in loud voices, not quite shouts, not much softer, but not really meant for the entire car to hear. She has something to say about how he shaves. He has something to say about the way she cooks turkey. She is wearing a yellow hat fifty years too late for yellow hats with small cloth daisies, and he has a cane that he whittled himself, and they are going from Bakersfield to Kansas to see her sister. He has something to say about that, too. Another passenger peels an orange, and another says he was attacked by dogs in Indonesia and is going home to get treatment, but the sores on his arms and face don't speak of dogs, and the gloss of fever means everyone for the most part leaves him alone, and what he wants most is a mug of tea, but because he is so tired, he decides to wait it out. Another passenger walks ahead for a smoke. A baby sleeps on her father's shoulder. The conductor reads a magazine and wishes he were elsewhere.

And America passes by like that in the night, when the windows show nothing but passenger reflections. It becomes New Mexico. It becomes Oklahoma. It becomes a train moving through a world made up of nothing but darkness punctuated by the little comma moon overhead. It becomes a train standing still as the world moves past. The arguing couple grows quiet, her head on his shoulder. The feverish boy sleeps and murmurs with feverish dreams. The baby is awake and watching her own reflection in the window, waving at her sweet new self as the night folds around us.

And so, in spring

   the rivers
      become sinuous
  and tempting,
green water
    dragging around
      fallen branches,
knocking little bits
   of earth away
     from the banks.
It may still be
  cold early and late,
  but at 2 p.m. it's hot
    and the water
     is cool and silky
and peaceful,
  but it isn't. That's wrong.
      The river isn't
       one danger,
but thousands—
   rapids,
     snags, currents,
       cold,
more snags, hidden currents,
   the fretful biting cold—
each one something
     never meant to happen
   to anyone,
but in April,
    in those new warm days,
    come the news reports

of drownings:
>a teenaged boy,
>an uncle who
>>jumped in
>>>to save some kid,
>two brothers, disappearing
>>so quietly everyone
>>>thought
>>>>they were off playing
>>>>>hide-and-seek,
>>>that they just didn't hear
>>>>when
>>>>>the olly olly in free
>>>>>>was called.

After Dry Lightning

Eight hundred fires are burning, and
we are all advised to stay indoors.
The sun is an electric pink disc.
You could almost hold its pink light
in your cupped hands, malleable as clay.
The black lizards of the forests
burrow deep. The air becomes
opaque, a world of ghosts,
and I, disobeying good advice,
run from backyard to front to see
the raging colors of sunset—odd,
fiery gift—and taste the smoke
on the back of my parched tongue.

Myriad Trees on Strange Mountains

The mountains appear to rise out of nothing,
the ground below them wallowing in fog,
insubstantial as sponge, indifferent as ground unseen,
unfelt can be.

The mountains appear to rise
out of nothing, their sides as steep and pleated
as the empress's nightgown.

The mountains
appear to rise out of nothing, standing together,
not touching, each one its self first, each one
part of the range sometime later.

Appearing to rise out of nothing,
the mountains are mysterious, holding
secrets under their stones, unraveling
tight-knit songs in their waterfalls.

The mountains appear to rise out of nothing,
topped by shocks of pine, windless and voiceless.
The dawn rises up the mountains, around the trees, but
under the branches, night clings with long fingers.

Night clings with long fingers and does not let go.

Solitary

The human brain cannot take a room alone
for long without beginning to unknit itself.

The long, dark pictures appear on the wall
both in front and behind, and the sound

of music from some floating elementary school—
the sound of fourth-grade recorders, isn't it?—

seems to be coming from the back left corner
of the tiny space. With eyes closed, the brain

tricks itself into seeing light. With ears stopped,
the voices come and go. The muffled footsteps' tic-tic

turns out to be your own heart. Try to recite
the Preamble, the Nicene Creed, the haiku

some teacher made you learn in junior high.
Make up your own haiku about the tic-tic

of hearts and footsteps, about the route
those footsteps might take around the house

you grew up in. Remember a story you read about
an innocent woman in solitary who wrote a novel

on the walls around her, memorizing what she'd
written each day, and then adding to it. She never

actually wrote anything down, but when she
was finally released the novel was in her mind,

each word word-linked to the next. The mind
knits and unknits itself, searches for available light.

Tear the button from the shirt and make a game
of finding it. The incoming dinner tray tolls like a bell.

July Fourth

You can't admit you hate fireworks
to the neighbors, who buy boxes and boxes
with names like Electrical Shock
and Flower Fountain, and invite you over
to watch. The spin, the sputter and hiss,
the cracks, the drifts of smoke going up
into the battered leaves of the tired trees.
The only time you speak all night is
to tell the story of a boy horribly burned
by fireworks, how people gawked and stared
at the ruin of his teenaged face. Your neighbors nod,
polite, and turn away to light another.
And then, they light what could become
your favorite if you didn't hate fireworks,
Pearls of the Orient. The way it bursts
into a white so bright and pure
and sends clean streaks of light
in a hundred directions at once.
A white like that can't possibly burn.
You want to run forward now
and hold those frenzied stars,
cupped in the palms of your hands.
But of course, you don't.
You stay in your plastic lawn chair and watch,
your eyes and the eyes of your neighbors
reflecting the hot birth of this temporary galaxy.
And then it's over and they weren't stars
at all, and the night is so full of smoke
from a thousand displays just like this
that the actual stars are no more
than photos in closed and dusty books.

Distraction, Furious and Brief

The Baptist church serves dinner at four, and the line
starts early, snakes around the shady side of the building.
Afternoon moves as slowly as summer heat lifts,
which is to say, it almost doesn't.
Bits of lives sink into the sidewalks.
Someone fixes a wheel on his cart of possessions.
Someone swigs something and passes it to his right.
And a woman in a sundress, colors of spring, crosses the street,
head up, chin out, confident the whole crowd's watching,
and some of them are as she stops, mid-crosswalk, hoisting her skirt high,
shaking her nakedness up and down, swinging her hips, her flesh
a mass of pink and bruise, head back, baring her teeth at the sky.
She turns and hip-bumps a furious circle dance
even as the light turns green, even as there are catcalls
and honking, even as some in the supper line look away
and some in the line shrug, and some keep watching
as she runs the rest of the way across the street, skirt up-up-up,
and the traffic moves on, and it's ten 'til, still hot, and
the long day's just the same as always.

Neville Bros. Service

On a morning after a night during which I did not sleep,
before a day in which I will answer a thousand questions,
at the end of which I will listen to news stories of a world
filled with complexities and connivings and grief upon grief,
it is then that I crave the clean lines of their building,
bricks laid against bricks, clean angle of the roofline,
twin garage doors, the way they fold left and right without hitching.
I yearn for the pure white behind the midnight blue letters—
that simplicity, that strength of purpose, that knowing—
the way the front doors and the windows work together,
each to their own, each respecting the whimlessness of the other.
Give me the glass bricks, heavy and cool, open only to light.
On a morning after a night before the day that closes with stories
about too many ends and seedy beginnings, I want to be the wind.
I want to be the wind flying over that building, blowing across that roof,
knowing nothing more heady than downdraft and tumble,
nothing more complicated than that brick and that mortar.

House for Sale

The house is loosened
    it's unbounded, unbound
by its walls and fences
    it's coming unfenced
joints gone all loosey-goosey
    boards missing
couches jumping ship or shipped out
    appliances falling out doors
they tumble and slide
    they crash and dent
they crash their object bodies
    onto the grass and the curb
into the gutter
    the house is junked
the junk that was housed
    is unhoused, half-orphaned
box spring skeleton rusts
    in droughted grass
mass of whatnot
    chair in a tree
there is a yellow chair
    in the gangly fig tree
hapless, hopeless
    helpless
this junked junk house
    this heap of forlorn
with its cataracted windows
    with its bike parts and
washing machine
    with Man A asleep
pillow/blanket/out like a light

    on a flatbed trailer
untrailed in the driveway
    with Man B awake
unshirted and surly
    harvesting washer parts
calling back into the house
    with its blinkless windows
with its doors loosely hinged
    and hanging, doors unslung
it's an open museum
    the ordinary made freakish
the toppled fridge
    props up the trailer
dining table next to motorcycle
    next to a deflated football
jukebox, tire pile, paint-can pyramid
    plastic box of Santa parts
next to the *for sale* sign
    this fixer upper, this great deal
this potential dream home
    for just the right buyer
for just the right stout-of-heart
    do-gooder, patron saint
of hard work and hopeful causes
    chair in a tree included

16 Reasons You Shouldn't Like Me (And I Don't Like Me Either)

I mine the cupboards of memory
And all I come up with is
A treasury of embarrassments.

*

The face in the store window
Is not the face in my imagination—
Too long, too crooked, too somber—
But it is the face of my disappointed face.

*

Fingernails: usually an afterthought—
Therefore, splitting; therefore, jagged.

*

Yes, a nap.
Each afternoon.
There's always housework,
But I'm always tired.

*

I am thoughtful to a fault
But I lack follow-through.
Your get-well card is unmailed,
But I did think of you.

*

I often bore myself with my own chatter.

*

Periodically, I listen to the news, and know
That in the wider world, none of the above matters.
And yet . . .

*

I need structure, little sets of building blocks,
Or I wander into anxiety's dank forests.

*

I cannot spell.
I dislike fractions.

*

Laziness is my little secret.
I cover it up with various reports
About penance and good works.

*

I am irredeemably freckled.
I have yearly checkups.
There is no cure.

*

Embarrassments include but are not limited to:
██████████████████████████████
██████████████████████████

(Consider this information redacted.)

*

When I'm not writing, I'm miserable.
This is also mostly true when I'm writing.

*

If you're my child, I need too much quiet,
Am too aware of dangers, write poems about you.

*

If you're my friend, I'm already worried
That I've offended you forever.

*

My attention span is evaporating—
Ocean, lake, pond, puddle, tiny . . . tiniest drop.

The Streets Are Quiet Here Early Mornings

Seagulls hunker in the schoolyard.
Juncos jabber and peck at the winter lawns.
Someone comes out in a bathrobe and socks
and picks up the paper. Inside,
there's coffee, buttered toast. Inside,
the radio's on, tuned to the news,
which is tuned to the latest despair.
O love, it's blind luck that we find ourselves here
and not in a land where souls lift themselves
daily out of rubble and ash. Dumb luck
that we have enough food, that we move freely,
read freely, that so far our child has survived.
We've done nothing to earn this.
And yet, here we are, ten thousand busy days ahead,
mostly ordinary, mostly safe in our tidy spaces,
mirrors reflecting back our slight discomfort.
The seagulls will rise into the coming days.
The juncos will head for the trees.
The radio news will keep reporting its lists of sorrows.
And we'll hold our breath that our luck will hold,
that we'll never make news at the top of the hour,
that there will always be nothing to see here.

A Boy Comes Toward You

he comes toward you
he has something in his hands
he's wearing a white shirt
he's black
his hood is up
he's white
his cap is on backward
he wears a black jacket
his hands are in his pockets
he's very tall
he's got headphones
he looks away
his jeans ride low
he's alone
what's in his hands
he smiles
both ears are pierced
a boy comes down the sidewalk
he winks
he's clean-cut
his shoes are dirty
he says *hey*
is it a coffee mug
he comes toward you
he looks you in the eye
you look him in the eye
down the sidewalk
he's eleven
he smiles
he has something in his hands
he's a thin boy
he's got an angry scar
he's nineteen
he doesn't smile
he doesn't make eye contact
he's chewing gum
he's smoking
he's holding the hand of a little girl
he looks straight ahead
he's Sikh, his hair wound in his *patka*
he's fourteen
one ear is pierced
his jacket is blue
you can't tell what's in his hands
is that a book under his arm
his hair is long
he says nothing
he's carrying something
he says please
he asks if he can pray for you
you look at what's in his hands
the prayer hangs in the air between you

Alphabet for a Mid-Sized City

Arable
The land around coaxes out
almonds, apricots, walnuts.
At 3 a.m., the call to irrigate.

Bone
We work our fingers to the bone.
We are bone-tired.
C'mon, throw the dog a . . .

Coonhounds
When sirens scream past,
the next-door dogs respond with all the sorrows
of the world in their voices.

Dalliance
Wind in the ash trees,
snail in the basil,
your hand in mine.

Ecogeographic
Hot afternoons, everything slows.
The air currents, the spin of the earth, the airplane
above moving so slowly it might drop into my hands.

Forb
Wild mustard grows in the ditches.
Green stem, yellow flower,
the bitter scent forecasts this ache or that.

Gimcrack
Lined up in the windows of that house
on the corner, each shiny object shooting back
sunlight, enough to blind a trespasser.

Headstones
Last night someone knocked them down,
broke them. The names of the dead mean
so little to some—some who need to be haunted.

Interlocution
"It sure is hot today."
    "I love the heat."
"Jeez, *mija*, you don't know what you love."

Jettison
In January, she'll cut back the roses after she drags
the Christmas tree out to the side of the road.
She's already penciled this in.

Kitchen
A bounty, an abundance of plums on the counter.
The ripe ones are splitting, juice pearling up,
even as we watch, even as we're breathless.

Longanimity
The lights start blinking just as you pull up
to the grade. The train has not yet appeared.
You open your window to hear it coming. You wait.

Matutinal
Morning comes out from behind the cedar tree.
Gray, then blue, then yellow, then gold. The hawks
call each other sweetheart. The routine begins again.

Nimbostratus
When we see them on the horizon, we cheer,
but quietly. We open the windows, we stand
on the porch, to smell the tang of pre-rain air.

Opine
The letters to the editor tell us this or that,
laud or outrage. Oh citizens! Either way,
the paper goes in the recycling bin after breakfast.

Pianissimo
The sound of the freeway from several blocks away.
The girl practicing piano with the windows closed.
The library with its efficiency, with the murmurs of all the books.

Quorum
Today's meeting is cancelled, as the members
of the Committee on the Importance of All Things
have hightailed it to the lake or are napping.

Reef
Under our feet, beneath the compacted soils,
encased in a vanished inland sea, are fossils
that won't be discovered for (possibly) ever.

Show-off
At night, I drive visitors to the glass factory.
Through the fence, through the half-open door,
we watch the white-hot glass drop into bottle shapes.

Trees
Winter wind can bulldoze down the almond trees.
The farmer counts them as they give up, as they keel,
as the wind takes even the blessed soil from the upturned roots.

Update
    "No, I'm pretty sure I know I love the heat."
"Well, *mija*, no one ever said you made sense."
    "Well, my friend, that is more true than you know."

Verdancy
From the new bridge, you see all the treetops
moving together in the breeze, so solid-looking
you could walk on them from here to Ceres.

Water
Also, *wait* and *watch*.
Also, *weather* and *warning*.
Also, *work* and *workers*, and *worn-out,* but not *worn down*.

X
Marks the spot where I ended up staying even after
declaring loudly that I did not want to end up here.
X marks the spot that's somehow become home.

Yes
So, because this became home, I began to say yes.
I am from here, yes. I like it here, yes. Not everything
is perfect, yes, but then nowhere is.

Zenith
The night of the meteor shower, I went out and looked
straight up at the bright pins of stars, some of them spinning
across the sky, most of them staying fastened to the night.

Avenue of the Giants, Auto Tour

Stop No. 8: The Drury-Chaney Loop

I would like to have Alice's little bottle now:
    "Drink me."
        And I would shrink down so that

the redwood sorrel would be a forest
    around me
        and I could look up through it—

the light green and underwatery—
    the sound of sorrel leaves trembling
        in the not-quite-wind, in the breath of the forest:

the sound of the bell as it leaves the bell—
    and I'd wander, hidden in my frail forest,
        until I came to a long-fallen log,

where the wood's gone spongy, and
    lie there for a little while. A fallen redwood
        can take five hundred years to decompose, and while doing so,

while the black beetles and the wood ants do their luxurious,
    necessary work, the old tree feeds the new.
        I'd lie there undisturbed, listening

to the movements of their insect jaws, and when ready,
    I'd nibble a tiny bit of sorrel stem, taste the tangy
        white juice, and rise again, my original size,

the path close at hand, other tourists
    'round the next bend, immense shadows
        shifting, shaking bits of forest
            out of my tangle of self.

Stop No. 7: Chandler Grove

My father-in-law is dead, but
here he comes from his walk
on the trail. It's a short walk,
and he's winded, but shining.
"The redwoods—" he says, looking
up. "The redwoods—" The sun
pours through them, mineral-like
and grand. My father-in-law leans
against a tree, raises his small black
camera. There's a click and he's gone,
and we are left with what's here:
the redwoods winding up and up, the canopy,
a great cantilevered cathedral ceiling,
and from somewhere up there:
wing-flutter and chattering,
a thrush we never see.

Stop No. 6: Dyerville Overlook

The afternoon light
sends out long shadows—
shadows of trees, of family,
shadow of bluff falling down on the river,
which bends out of shadow, silver as a trout.

The Forest Service signs tell a thing or two—
how the bluff is thirty feet of fill,
remnants of the washed-away town—
doorsills and enameled sinks,
rail ties and tires and window glass,
the crushed porches of Main Street—
not the purpose they were meant to serve,
but still serving a purpose.

Beneath our shadows,
the bluff creaks and groans
like the stairs the mayor of Dyerville climbed
on his lonesome way to bed.

The Dyerville Giant

When a tree falls in a forest,
a tree like that, anyway,
with all those years ringing it,
having sprouted out of the soft earth
before Jesus was even a spark
in his Father's bright eye—
when a tree like that falls,
it cracks and echoes so that
even the gnats careening
in the sun near the creek
take pause. And when this tree
fell, the crash was like trains colliding.
The ground inhaled and held
its breath, waiting for impact.
The sound rolled through the forest
and made salamanders hide
in their damp burrows. It thundered
like a train wreck, and so
the townsfolk drove out
to the trestle to see the havoc,
while the fine silt of redwoods
rose and then settled
in the forest behind them.

Stop No. 5: Mahan Plaque

And so the lesson is this:
prison is still prison
even if the prison happens to be
among redwoods and owls,
up a gravel road lined with
the soft arms of ferns,
with a view of the mountains
and before them the ravine
through which, you've been told,
a river runs, flat and silver, toward
the sea. But the river doesn't matter,
and the mountains and the owls
don't matter. A prison is still a prison.
So here's your wanted poster, taped
to a redwood log, your eyes,
bleak and young, looking out
at the scenery. Some of the tourists
read the Mahan Plaque, and some
read your poster under trees
that render all of us impossibly small,
that make our voices into murmurs
drifting out and away in the breeze,
which, high in the treetops,
sounds like the highway, and
the highway, you know,
leads toward home.

Nature Walk

The fern fronds glow with a clean, green light,
and I lift one and point out the spores, curled
like sleep on the back, the rows so straight,
so even, that I might be convinced of Providence
at this moment. My daughter is seven.
She looks at the spores, at the leaf, at the plant,
at this wise, wide forest we are in, and sighs
at my pointing out yet another Nature Fact.
But look, I say, *each one is a baby ready*
to grow. Each one can become its own fern.
But she is already moving down the path
toward the bridge and whatever's beyond.

Stop No. 4: Weott

The town is gone, washed out in
the Christmas Flood of '64,
when the river
in which they fished,
in which they swam,
in which they paddled tin canoes—
the south fork of the Eel—
next to which they built bonfires,
next to which they kissed
while the moon kissed the river,
down which they sent logs to the mill,
over which they built the bridge,
next to which they built the town
described as "bustling" that December
when it rained for days and the river
rose thirty-three feet above the highway
and took what it wanted, and
it wanted nearly everything, and left just
the sidewalks, which you can still
find if you look hard enough
and are schooled in the ways
of persistence and brambles and memory.

Drive-Thru Tree, Myersville

Forgive me, America.
I do not want to drive through a tree.

I would not mind being somehow inside a tree,
a part of the tree, to feel the soft hum of treeness,

the click as one ring solidifies and another
begins its history. But to drive my car

through a tree violates some unspoken rule
of etiquette, seems as terribly awkward

as showing up uninvited to a wedding
of a couple, one of whom you used to date.

I don't know if the tree minds, America.
I don't know if it cares about being

a roadside attraction, but I can't help
but think it would rather be left alone

with its birds and its sunlight, nursing
its bright new growth. I can't help but think

the tree more content if the cars were over there,
on the highway, moving quickly somewhere else.

Stop No. 3: Visitors' Center/ Burlington Campground

The interruption of the parking lot,
the hard glare after the cool shadows
of the woods, the herds of camper vans
and SUVs, the hunched groups
clutching bags of souvenirs, the way
heat wavers up from the pavement—

but the promise of more quiet
just down the road, the promise of
a creek in the July noon, the promise
of walking through the deep green
on a path almost overgrown
with sorrel, their yellow flowers—

Keep driving.

Between Stops

Windows rolled down,
we swoosh by the trees,
each one soaring up
and farther up in its coat
of thick bark. We poke
our heads out the windows
and look at the canopy.
Green flies above us,
a glorious stuttering of
sun and shadow on our faces.
She laughs, and her laugh
sails up and trills around
the osprey nests and
shimmers—can you hear it?—
in the tops of these trees.

Stop No. 2: Bolling Grove

Each ecosystem makes its own set of rules:
coordinates for this, logarithms for that.
In this canopy, at the axis of x (being the limb)
and y (being the trunk), the years accumulate
their treasures of fallen needles and twigs.
The mat builds and builds. The air grows
more humid above it, with its spongy
corridors, with its microbial cities. Salamanders
move in with their small possessions to feast.
The hawks land and survey the silvery distance.
And a dogwood tree grows ownerless and lovely,
two hundred feet up, its roots clenched tight in the limb
of the redwood. The arboreal salamanders
live out their lives up here, their small
black feet never once touching the ground.
In the afternoon breeze that carries in the fog,
the dogwood claps out a soft applause,
exponents for continuing this existence.

Stop No. 1: Franklin K. Lane Grove

    The road is forty miles, then it ends here
and sloughs us back onto the freeway
        going southward—
                south—southward.

But *starflower! trillium!* the heart sings,
    remembering their shy ways,

and the blood hums the green
        and liquid songs of ferns,

    and the skin relishes the cool of the fog,

and the soul breathes
        slowly in and out and in,
    savoring its finite cache
            of redwood-flavored air,

and the mind, in its pragmatism, steels itself
            against homesickness,
    placing word next to word,
        beginning to consider the poem.

Neighborhood

Neighborhood

Houses of a certain vintage, early mid-century,
a little time-worn maybe, a little down-in-the-mouth.
Never mind, though. Never mind. This is home, this street
with its collections of plant life and human secrets.

Fraxinus velutina glabra 'Modesto': our ash trees.
Too many, too close, and one sick tree becomes many sick trees.
In spring, the new leaves curl and fall, a sudden yellow-green carpet.
More leaves unfurl, sparser, clinging hard to the exhausted twigs.

On some mornings outside, the smell of bacon; on others, just fog.

...

Every house has a dog or two, but it's the cats' dominion.
Early mornings, they line up and sit in the street,
sentries for the coming day. A car eases its way along.
The cats don't move. They will brook no disturbance.

Each house is filled with stories, mostly unknown.
The woman with the crutches has had crutches forever,
and no one has ever seen the resident of the pink house,
though sometimes the plants on the porch are rearranged.

Our neighbor shoots at cats with a rubber-band gun, a futile effort.

...

The day we moved in, Mr. Watson came to shake our hands, and
Anita came with a hand trolley, and the woman from across the street
came out and told us hello and that she was the caretaker
    for a woman who had just died and the family
was selling and now she had to move and wasn't that a shame.

Down the block is a farmhouse, nothing like the others (not a certain vintage).
The curtains are drawn. The car in the driveway is flat-tired and faded.
Yet every night, the lights inside come on.
Every night, the TV antenna on the roof hums a little in the wind.

The backyard plum tree, festooned in white petals, hums along with spring's bees.

. . .

Houses of a certain vintage, all described as modest.
Houses with detached garages, with old-growth boxwoods.
That one's a rental, and the last family moved away without a word.
That one's been in the family for three generations; everyone talks at once.

Green is a changeable color.
The green of the ash trees is not the same as the green of lawns,
not the same as the green of the buddleia,
not the same as the green of kitchen paint circa 1947.

We plant a Japanese maple in the front yard in case the ashes die off.

. . .

We found buried trinkets in the backyard when we moved here:
a yellow metal toy truck, wheels missing, some marbles, and
two ceramic frogs that fit in the palm of one hand. Flip them over
and view their anatomically correct human genitalia if you'd like.

Pam lived next door growing up, lived in the house across
the street when she married, and hopscotched into the house over there
when the kids were small. She's lived all her life on the same street.
She's known the taste of plums from a certain tree forever.

The backyard dovecote, here when we bought the house,
    was gone when we moved in.

. . .

Once, we found love notes torn to pieces and scattered up
and down the length of the block. We rode our bikes back and forth,
picking up the pieces, and patched the letters back together.
Many pieces were missing, but the heartbreak was not.

A dead bird on the lawn. The girl counts the pieces.
One head, one tail, one other. A large feather quivers in the grass.
Her dad will clean it up. Her mom will write a poem.
The neighborhood cats will lick their cruel chops.

Sometimes from across the alley, we hear a family fighting a hard fight.

. . .

Henrietta overwaters her lawn, even during droughts.
The water spills down the sidewalk, fills the gutter with a little river,
creates a little reservoir where roots have heaved up the pavement.
The mosquitoes say thanks with their luckless mouths, but no one else does.

Sometimes, ham-fisted tragedy shows up, takes a seat at the curb.
Once, a boy died on the sidewalk when something in his brain shattered
and bloomed. His father shut the house and moved away. The grass
grew tall. The grass grew tall and bent in the sometime-breeze.

The hollyhock row between front yards is a curtain between two worlds.

...

Each year in February, the magnolia bursts into pink exuberance.
Each flower catches the light and prisms it back into the world
until we are reminded again of the impermanence of everything. Inevitably,
there's a storm and the flowers shed themselves into the wind.

One house, unwanted and failing, was empty of people for months,
but filled still with possessions, the soupspoons and pencil nubs of family.
Vandals broke in and took what they wanted, even the back fence,
    even the doorknobs.
They left a little mouse figurine in the window, though,
    left it staring out at the street.

At the liquor store two blocks away, someone was shot and killed.

...

Mr. Watson walked several miles a day, cane in hand, just in case.
He tended his blue truck and his dog and his wife. In his left pocket,
memories of the Devil's Highway, of the tanks he drove; in his right pocket,
snapshots of the grandkids and the great-grandkids and his wife and Tiger the dog.

This is a neighborhood absent of squirrels.
It's the cats maybe, their persistent hungers.
There are birds, though, in their universe of trees,
and there are rats, though we don't like to think of them.

Our neighbor brings us Mexican pastries: empanadas, *conchas, campechanas*.

. . .

Our girl's only a few days old when Mrs. Watson,
whose knees are bad, calls and says she hasn't seen the baby.
We bundle her up and go, of course. We watch while she cradles
our daughter, introduces herself, saying, "Just call me Grandma Watson."

Lev killed the rat with a stomp of his boot.
Lev wrote his name in the wet cement at someone else's house.
Lev hunted a bear and laid it in the driveway for us all to see.
Lev coos to his granddaughter, lets her small, new fist curl around his finger.

I cannot remember the caretaker's name, or the name of the boy who was killed.

. . .

The world's oldest dog lived on the corner, his face gray, his back crooked.
We loved him and his sideways gait, and when he died, we wished he hadn't.
Now, in his place, a parrot tears at the night with squawks made of acid and chalk,
and that bird will live longer than we do.

Sylvie tells stories when we ask her and sometimes when we don't.
In this house, a sex offender. In this house, a conspiracy theorist.
In this house, shelves of canned goods and car parts and every size screw.
In this house, at all hours, the strained sounds of banjos and typewriters.

We plant a fig tree too, and a cherry and a lemon and a lime.

. . .

All day we can hear the hum of traffic two streets away.
All night we can hear the hum of traffic two streets away.
Sometimes we can hear the train on the other side of the freeway,
making itself known in a voice as alone as a monk's.

The city arborists come every couple of years to cut the mistletoe
out of the ashes. They cut some out, and they leave some in the trees
in their radial, berried bunches. In December's gray mornings,
the silvery leaves look like galaxies in the universe of branches.

Our daughter painted her hand green and stamped her print on the driveway.

. . .

In the third year of drought, a family lets their lawn die.
Among twenty green lawns is a lawn
the color of crunching heat and mountain lion.
The neighbors try not to notice as they adjust their sprinklers.

Some nights, that brazen moon shines directly into the bedroom,
but how can anyone shut the blinds to moonlight?
How can anyone shut out the color silver, the way it makes the world
into a photograph, black and white and still?

Just before sunrise, a bird . . . not singing, exactly. You couldn't call it that.

. . .

And there are the hawks nesting in the lopsided cedar,
and jays and mockingbirds, and rock doves that mate on the patio.
There are hummers that sit their whirring selves on the wire for just a second,
and phoebes who swoop from their mud-and-straw home to chase us away.

In this house, no door closes tightly.
In this house, the foundation has shifted.
At this house, the fence is shored up with extra boards.
At this house, the lion statues on the porch are shedding their white paint.

Some neighbors move away, but not before spotting Mars from their backyard.

. . .

The neighborhood poet looks out the window; someone mows his grass,
leaves swirl on the driveway, a red car drives by.
The day's heat is picking up; it'll be 94 by noon.
The poet sighs and wonders what to make of this.

There was a fancy wrought-iron seat around the cedar at the sorrowful house,
the house with the forlorn mouse figurine. The cedar grew and the bench
tipped and broke apart, rusting itself into pieces. Then one day it was gone.
The cedar may miss its companion, may wonder at the absent embrace.

I kept the shredded love notes in a mason jar. They did not regrow
    their missing pieces.

. . .

And as for the plants that take over . . . the wisteria, the vinca,
the ivy, the evening primrose, the ponytail grass, the jasmine.
Sometimes we fight them with our trimmers and shovels,
sometimes we let them have their greedy way.

Consider for a moment all the beds in all the houses,
made or unmade, duvets or blankets, one pillow
or two. Consider the softened spots in the mattresses,
the dreams loosed into the darkened corners.

Mrs. Watson's gone to assisted living, but Paulette mails her a card every week.

. . .

The child thought her backyard a forest of fruit trees and roses;
the lawn stretched on for an eternity. A trip to the back gate might take
all day. When she's grown, the size of the yard will surprise her.
Has the place always been so small? Have the gate hinges always been so rusted?

The ash trees' roots push the sidewalks askew. The streetlights flick on
at a precise stage of dusk. A car door slams, a screen door slams,
and someone is home. The cats clean their paws in anticipation of night.
There's a season, then another. We're already awaiting the magnolia's next bloom.

The houses (a certain vintage) breathe in, breathe out; the hawks drift
     home on their warmth.

. . .

The Moon Rises, Almost Full

New Life with Bees and Fire

Woman gives birth, fights off bees, starts wildfire in Northern California
—*LA Times* headline, June 30, 2015

My mother's head was wreathed in nonsense.
My mother's head was wreathed in the shadows of owls
And sometimes in stars, a million winks around her.
My mother's head was wreathed in sweat, in tears.
My mother's head was wreathed in bees.
Their buzzing was the second language I learned.
My mother's head hung low when she slept.
My mother's head was wreathed in regret.
She whispered in the night, *no phone, no water, four apples to eat,*
Stupid short-cut through the woods, over the river
And through the woods to grandmother's house, she sang
And she whispered. Her head hung low when she slept.
Her breathing was the first language I learned.
My mother's head was wreathed in apple breath.
My mother's head was wreathed in daylight, then moonlight.
My mother's head was beautiful and terrible in sorrow.
My mother's head was close to mine, close to mine;
Her breath was warm and soft and apple-riddled.
My mother's head was wreathed in daylight again and again.
My mother's head was filled with getaway plans:
Walk out, float out, fly out on the wings of owls.
My mother's head was wreathed in nonsense, in tears.
My mother's head was wreathed in smoke. My mother's head
Was wreathed in smoke and in flames that rushed and crackled.
Fire was the third language I learned.
My mother's head close to mine, her lips close to mine,
Breathing and breathing with the smoke all around her.
My mother's head was wrapped in relief like stars
When the rescuers came. They tamped out the fire,
They took us away from the owls and shadows,
The bees, the flames, the winking stars,
And we began to begin the beginning again.

7 Fieldstone Drive

Up these stairs, the children's rooms.
At the top of the stairs, on this wall,
the painting of Jesus the Shepherd
with pink-cheeked children, adoring sheep.
Behind this door is the blue room.
Behind that door is the bright white tub.
Behind the door over there is the pink room.
In the pink room stands an old desk.
In the old desk is a simple drawer.
In the simple drawer is a leaf
picked up in the schoolyard,
carried home in a pocket.
In this leaf, yellow and red,
already drying: a dream ending,
a world beginning, leaf veins
like small roads leading
away, away, away
from here.

My Father Begins to Disappear

My father has no fat on his bones.
Blue veins run the lengths of his stringy muscles,
down his wrists and across his hands,
a foundering delta, a delta silting itself in and disappearing.
His hands are bone and skin, even the palms gone slack.
His nails are brittle and crack for no reason.
Every day there is less of him.
He used to say that when the time came, we should
set him adrift at sunset to find his own Valhalla.
We would laugh, say *Yes, of course*. But now,
each day bringing that time closer, my father
says less and less. Even the words he wants to say
get caught on his tongue and lost . . . he shakes his head *never mind*.
His hips hurt. Bruises don't heal. The house is never warm enough.
Home from a visit, I realize that I barely spoke with him.
He's the shade in the corner, almost a photograph of himself,
almost a discrete set of memories. He's becoming past tense.
Dad on a swing in Cape Cod, blowing soap bubbles for me.
Dad running us around the house on his shoulders.
Dad dancing, pretend debonair, in the kitchen.
Dad at his favorite marina, smiling,
not one of the docked boats behind him
prepared to take him aboard.

Photo of Two Sisters, 1975

Who roller-skates in early winter?
Sycamore leaves littering the sidewalk,

each a hazard added to the hazard of root bumps
and sidewalk lines, but there we are in roller skates.

You in your Big Bird hat, grinning that wide grin,
and me in the fat blue parka Mom made from a kit

the year Dad was in Alaska. Remember how we'd pull
downy feathers from the seams? The world around

us is winter-crazed and dying, but there you are
in your goofy yellow-red hat, and there I am

in that downy-blue parka, and we're holding hands,
and the house behind us looks warm, and

we're going roller-skating in early winter. Who cares
about the cold or the darkening sky? It doesn't matter,

because this is evidence, captured on film.
This is us being happy together.

Owl Sighting

Each morning we'd search
for the small pellets of bone and fur and tail
in the scruffy grass under that palm: unfortunate
mice who'd become her solitary meal.
And we'd find them . . .

                    bone turned almost the color
of the late-summer grass, fur scraps the color
of the neglected dirt. Odd treasures, but proof
our ghost was up there, in her palm palace, proof that
she'd come home again.

                    And that was what we wanted.
Hungry from all the nights we could hear her call,
the long whoo-whoo bouncing off stucco and asphalt
and down to us, who'd point and wonder
if she were here or in that tree there,
until finally,

      we'd make ourselves still under a sky gone
so deeply blue you could taste it on your lips, and
we'd wait, the grass crunching under our shoulders, and
wait, the moon rising from behind the mountain, and wait,
knowing we'd be called in soon, and wait, holding our
breath and then

                                  she'd launch from her nest all at once. No rustling
to alert us, not even the shiver of moonlit fronds. And for a split-second
she'd be closer than any of us would have liked. She'd
launch herself out to the west and away and away,
this massive winged shadow,

                              and if one of us blinked,
she'd be gone, and we'd only know by the sharp
intakes of breath around us, and if we saw her go,
even then we'd wonder if we'd dreamed it;
we'd doubt what we'd seen

                    because
it seemed impossible, this kind of beauty,
living here in our tree, in our yard, so lovely
in the sudden moment of her departure, this
shadow bird, this twilight ghost, this remedy
against another cloistered suburban night.

Later Stages

Look at Mr. Ken, she says
to her chattering girl,
and there is my father,
with his hands clapped over his ears,
with his face screwed up in pain,
with his mind a swirl of shout and clatter
and with no ability to sort them out.
Now just look at Mr. Ken, she scolds.
The child looks and looks away.
She cannot understand the way the mind works
and then doesn't. Just as my father cannot
understand why the words fly in
like small, sharp-voiced birds
and fly out again just as fast,
some of them leaving shadows
and some of them leaving nothing at all.

Empty Garden

This is not a metaphor for anything.
It is what it is, this garden,
empty as a plate. The sage
and the rosemary gone. Lemon balm
pulled up clump by clingy clump.
Lavender dug up with an old spade.
The errant olive tree pulled out by the roots.
Even the lamb's-ear, though loved,
had to go, as it never dried, and rotted
from the middle out each winter.

Now, the garden is a dirt display,
a land unimproved, unlovely, dirt
clods cuddling dirt clods, their
double-dug selves crumbling a little
at the edges under a sun made to sap
water from rock. And the question
becomes what to do, what to do. The gardener
has no plans, can't think what plants, isn't reading
books to plant plans in her middling mind.

Never mind, she thinks, never mind.
Let the worms and the weeds have their day.
Let the absent metaphor rustle in the absent leaves

Miró's *Women and Bird in the Moonlight*

But the bird looks like an infant
launched toward the asterisk stars.
Round face browning in the blue light,
unsmiling, eyes wide open. Launched
quite deliberately out of the dense world
of mother and dog.

There is the dog looking skyward
at the infant Icarus, whose arms are spread wide.
And there is the mother turning to see
her child, caresses already boxed
and stored inside her.

She can't quite believe that's her baby,
whose eyes reflect the stars and
who won't return, who will not return
in any recognizable form.

Flood

If the water rose—
If the water rushed in—
If the water crept in like a draft—
If the water crashed down—
If the water weren't water but mud,
slurry of tree trunks and boulders.
If the water came in under the door,
merrily at first, then staying, becoming crankier,
picking at the wallpaper, undoing the draperies.
If the water licked at our toes, our knees, our hipbones—
If the water played with the ends of our hair, our eyelashes—
If the water pressed into our throats, entered our ear canals—
If the water smelled like the bitter end of days—
If the water gave off the rank of rotted meat—
If the water wasn't the color of sky, but of earth—
If the water wasn't the color of earth, but
the color of the insides of nightmares—
If there isn't a warning—
If there isn't any time—
If the call comes too late—
If the attic's too shallow,
the roof too weak—
If there's no wood for a raft—
If the oars are missing, and
the drownings, my darling,
have begun—

The Big One

The article about earthquakes scares everyone,
    even those who don't want to admit it.
No one cannot be scared of the world
    turning to liquid beneath them.
Forget the jars and books falling off the shelves.
    (The raspberry jam! The Whitman!)
Forget the little explosions of wineglasses
    as they hit the counter.
The fact is that parts of seemingly solid land
    will liquefy and churn beneath our feet,
beneath the car tires, beneath the foundations
    we thought of as permanent.
Two minutes—three minutes—four minutes:
    length equals intensity, and
intensity undoes the laces that hold
    the crotchety ocean in its place.
And my brain balks at thinking about that:
    about the ocean leaving its bed
to push mine and yours and everyone's
    into some other county,
into some other otherness, not a bed,
    not a topography I recognize in sight.
Word is, the Big One's overdue by years,
    a tardy party crasher,
and even as I type this, I'm saying goodbye
    to certain grasses and bridges,
to a couple of restaurants,
    to certain unnamed individuals,
to certain stretches of beach
    that I've known and I've loved.
Buddha comes in handy here—

    lessons about impermanence,
about letting go, about living in the moment—
    but I am almost positive that
the moment we'll live most intensely
    is when the sirens start wailing,
when the earth starts shaking,
    when we realize the Big One is now.

Birdsong

The eleven varieties
               of mountain birds
sing and sing their songs—
    drifting songs—
        aching songs—
songs punctuated with crickets and pine nuts
    and a certain amount of wistful mystery,
and people have stopped to listen,
    to decipher the meanings
of trills
    and crescendos
        and chirps
           and the little silences between—
but all eleven varieties know the songs
    are nothing. They're nothing:
just notes and trills and chirps
    just because, just because—
and knowing that, five of the eleven varieties
    take up laughing instead,
which to the foolish human ear
    sounds like just
a different song.

Father-Daughter Dance: A Ghazal

Once, he tried to teach me how to use a slide rule,
but I never learned and now he has forgotten, this stricken father.

The television replaces any need for conversation.
So now we speak "police drama" and "sit com," me and my father.

He wants to go to the hardware store, asks where the wood is. Once there,
he knows he wants to build, but can't remember what, this man who is my father.

Another slow walk to the car, cane in one hand, my wrist in the other.
I will feel his grip for hours after, this ache from my father.

In the long afternoon, are you thinking of what might have been?
A different decision maybe, a little less emotion, Father?

We do not look at each other when I clean his dentures, soak them,
brush them, hand them back. I do not look at the once and future face of my father.

At three in the morning, he coughs, he murmurs in his sleep.
Across the hall, I am awake, listening to this man of diminishing returns, my father.

And what to do with my emotions? Stitch up, button down this anger, love, pity,
this compassion, this grief by seconds and inches, all for my wayward father?

No wish, no prayer, no miracle, no abracadabra magic
will replace this gray man with the man who used to be my father.

Dad, you aren't sure who I am, call me by other names, but
some things are unchanging, and I am, flailing and unfailingly, your daughter.

Astronomy for Mother and Daughter

I love you to the moon and back,
she says, and I say to Venus and back,
and she says to Mercury and back,
and I say to Neptune and back,
and she says to Pluto and back,
and we take a moment because
in our hearts, Pluto will always be a little planet
far away, an underdog in the outersphere . . .
but then I say to the edge of the universe and back,
which ends the game, since in her mind
the universe is finite and solid, a vast playground
of stars and planets and nebulae lit from within.
And I don't explain that the universe is expanding,
that there is an edge, and that it is farther
away all the time, like a dream remembered
when you woke but that slips more from your grasp
each moment you're awake. I don't tell her yet
that the universe is growing and that if you get that far
there is no coming back, just a continuing, just
a moving onward, outward into the unknown,
into the newly created, and that even though
it is almost beyond understanding, my moonstruck one,
my stargazer, that is how much I love you.

Letter to My Husband Far Away

The house is not empty without you.
It thrums and bumps, the walls relax and sigh.
The water heater dutifully comes on, rumbles
with heat, waiting for your shower to start.
How many times today have I heard
your truck in the driveway, the floor creak
with your step, felt your breath against
the back of my neck. At least that often,
I've turned to tell you something,
or hand you a piece of cheese or plum,
but it's two more days until you return.
It's just me in this room, with this plum,
with this good fortune, with this far-flung love.

Road Song, North on 99

We are hushed
    and sequenced
we're the road
    we're the fence
mountains in the distance
    cuddled up
each peak has a name
    we don't know
as we don't know the names
    of the husk-dry grasses
we are hushed
    we are sequenced
first this town, then the next
    long, blank betweens
what's not predictable
    is which store is shuttered
or which graffiti
    has faded to shadow
we are hushed by the heat
    sequenced by the map
led and humbled
    by the cracked and patched
by the pavement
    cracked and patched
we're hushed
    we're slung-low
fence posts slap by
    count and lose count
swerve for the dead dog
    swerve for the breakdown
we're hushed and sequenced

    we're low-slung and low
there's cloud glower
    there's lightning without rain
dust spins itself a frenzy
    a tipping tower
the radio gets only fuzz
    since the antenna broke
we're hushed, we're silent
    the road a throat song
        thrumming beneath us

My Autopsy

Please start with my left arm, between the twin bones
radius and ulna. Neither has ever been jealous of the other.

Instead, they work in harmony, as I was often unable to do.
So, please start here, and when you examine, don't be surprised

that you find those bones not as ivory as you imagined, but
quite possibly some shade of blue, and inscribed with the many names

I meant to call my children (Francesca, Samuel, Coco, etc.)
if I had had more children, but conditions what they are, this is

no time for regret. Once done with the left arm, once satisfied
with the narrow blood vessels and the sinew and the marrow,

once reminded of the divine in the way the elbow brings together
the harmonious bones and the brute strength of the humerus

with such grace, please move on to the right thigh. No god was born
of this thigh, and please don't make faces at the cellulite. It has been

with me a while and has never apologized for itself, and I won't
start now. Just move aside its pretty yellow-white clouds and admire

the fine rafts of muscle, laid out like the butcher's best offerings.
Admire the quite majestic femur, the king of bones, long and solid

as we all intend life to be, how it soars up to the hip and down
to the knee, and breaking it seems nearly impossible, though we

know this isn't true; we're all fragile as china cups
when you come down to it, we silly creatures, without exoskeleton

or much inner strength. Ah, me. Now, turn your attention to
my throat. Yes, the larynx is rigid and arrogant besides, but many

of us are larynx-like in these ways. Please look for everything left unsaid
gathered there, like goodies in a picnic basket, waiting

for discovery and expression: the thank-you I meant to give the neighbor
for her gift of banana bread, the telling off I meant to give . . . I can't remember,

I'm sure it was important, the secret always on the tip of my tongue, and
where I put the key to the garage, but never mind now, you'll find it, and

it's all so mundane anyhow. Is there an organ to process the mundane?
If there is, it must be enlarged and perhaps was the cause of my surprise demise.

In your examination, please keep an eye out for the black box (actually orange)
that undoubtedly recorded the warning signals, the systems failures, and

my last words, which I hope were witty, but probably were not.
Possibly it is hidden behind the pancreas or is lodged in the pink-gray ravines

of my brain, along with snippets of books I've read, pieces of recipes, and
hapless bits of trivia (Barbara Stanwyck's mother was run over

by a city bus), but yes, I digress and digress again, fall into myself and
forget myself. And you have work to do; please continue with the task

at hand, unless it is my hand you'd like to work on next.
I'd prefer that you left them both alone. I have my

reasons. And also my eyes: hazel dims to dull brown after death, so leave
them be, but here: your consolation prize, my examiner, the lungs are yours,

funny balloons, and the heart if you want it, maligned and clichéd though
it is. Use the sharpest scalpel and weigh and catalog what must be weighed

and cataloged. In the middle of me, perhaps you'll find a small, radiant moon,
a reverse and inner galaxy. The Babylonians believed the liver was the seat

of the soul. Poor Babylonians, long gone, unautopsied. No reason given
for the deaths of all those unremembered. It comes down to that,

doesn't it? We all want answers, reasons, unfurled before us like a good novel,
like a novel that will be read and kept on the shelf for a long, long time,

like a story that will be told and retold, each of us an Odysseus. So,
open me up, kind examiner. I, too, want to be a story no one will ever forget.

This Sweet Haphazard

No one calls this town pretty.
Not with the dusty oleanders off the freeway
and the ragged fence boards of backyards
propped up with two-by-fours, and
the canals with their twin lies of slow and safe,
and the ash trees, dead branches dangling, and
the large, pale no-one's-home houses and
the foreclosed houses and the small houses
with their carefully tended geranium borders,
with the plum trees gone overripe and sticky.
No one calls this town pretty, with the heat
rippling off the parking lots and the sighs
of aunts and uncles sitting in the shade of garages
filled with cars that were once meant to go places,
and the church marquee scolding that
Jesus Did Not Read Porn, and the swarms
of mosquitoes buzzing the standing water
from the leaking sprinkler heads in the park.
And yeah, no one calls this town pretty
as the creek laps at its share of shopping carts,
and the untended grasses bleach dry by April,
and the public pools are mostly closed,
but the sky here turns indigo on summer nights,
and the hummingbird chases the sparrow
from the feeder, and the kids on the soccer field
run as fast as kids anywhere, oblivious
to the town around them, because after all,
it isn't so bad. It's an okay town.
We know where all the roads go,
and we know where to get good coffee,
and we know what time the train pulls through.

We know too we're more than soil, more than sky,
more than what you've read in the news,
and no, it isn't pretty, but we still live here, and
tonight the moon will rise, almost full,
over this sweet haphazard of home.

Notes

"Myriad Trees on Strange Mountains" was inspired by a painting entitled *A Myriad of Trees on Strange Peaks*, probably by Li T'ang, early twelfth century, *in Chinese Painting*, compiled and written by James Cahill (Editions d'Art Albert Skira, 1960).

Neville Bros. Service is an auto repair shop on Needham Street in Modesto, California.

The poems in "Avenue of the Giants, Auto Tour" were inspired by a trip down the Avenue of the Giants highway (Highway 101) in Northern California. Our trip was taken driving north to south, Stops No. 8 to 1, hence the order of the poems. "Stop No. 5: Mahan Plaque" refers to High Rock Conservation Camp No. 32, a detention center off the Avenue of the Giants.

The painting by Joan Miró, *Women and Bird in the Moonlight* (1949), is currently in the Tate collection.

"Flood" was written in response to Hurricane Katrina and to the 2010 Arkansas Campground floods.

"The Big One" was written in response to "The Really Big One" by Kathryn Schulz in *The New Yorker*, July 20, 2015.

The title of "My Autopsy" was borrowed from a poem of the same title by Michael Dickman.

Acknowledgments

Huge thanks to the following publications in which these poems appeared, sometimes in different versions: *California Quarterly*: "Astronomy for Mother and Daughter"; *Clade Song*: "Birdsong"; *The Dirty Napkin*: "America by Train"; *In Posse*: "My Father Begins to Disappear"; Modesto Art Museum (limited-edition chapbook): "Neville Bros. Service"; *Modesto Bee*: "And so, in spring"; *More Than Soil, More Than Sky: The Modesto Poets* (Quercus Review Press): "This Sweet Haphazard" and "Owl Sighting"; *Packinghouse Review*: "Owl Sighting" and "Empty Garden"; *Quercus Review*: "My Autopsy" and "July Fourth"; *Sow's Ear Review*: "Flood"; *Spillway*: "Red Velvet Mite"; *Stanislaus Connections*: "The Streets Are Quiet Here Early Mornings"; *Toyon Review*: "Photo with Two Sisters"; *Up the Staircase Quarterly*: "Stop No. 4"; *West Marin Review*: "After Dry Lightning"; *Wherewithal*: "16 Reasons You Shouldn't Like Me (And I Don't Like Me Either)" and "A Boy Comes Toward You"; *Zócalo Public Square*: "Old Mill Cafe."

Thank you to the friends who gave advice that helped shape this book, including Gerald Fleming, Lynne Knight, Murray Silverstein, Helen Wickes, and all the members of Sixteen Rivers Press. Thank you to Tom Portwood, Stella Beratlis, and especially Linda Scheller, for their good advice and kind support. Thanks to my husband, Joe Orlando, my first and best reader; to the poetry community of Stanislaus County for their support and enthusiasm; to my wonderful neighbors; to Marian Martino who was willing to jump in and work on this book with me; and to my daughter, Sophie, for putting up with it all.

Sixteen Rivers Press is a shared-work, nonprofit poetry collective
dedicated to providing an alternative publishing avenue for
Northern California poets. Founded in 1999 by seven writers,
the press is named for the sixteen rivers that flow into San Francisco Bay.

SAN JOAQUIN · FRESNO · CHOWCHILLA · MERCED · TUOLUMNE · STANISLAUS
CALAVERAS · BEAR · MOKELUMNE · COSUMNES · AMERICAN · YUBA · FEATHER
SACRAMENTO · NAPA · PETALUMA